A PARABLE ABOUT THE

KING

BETH MOORE

ILLUSTRATIONS BY BEVERLY WARREN

Broadman & Holman Publishers   Nashville, Tennessee

Cover and interior design: Robin Black, UDG / DesignWorks, Sisters, Oregon

Published in 2003 by Broadman & Holman Publishers, Nashville, Tennessee

DEWEY: CE
SUBHD: GOD—FICTION \ LOVE—FICTION \ PARABLES

ISBN 0-8054-2679-5

1 2 3 4 5   07 06 05 04 03

TO PEYTON AND SAVANNAH,

Princesses indeed—

What fun to watch you grow from across the aisle

of our church. I'm so proud of you.

I love you,

Miss Beth

ONCE UPON A TIME a young princess became angry with her father, the King. The King had required her obedience to clean her room, but she had countless servants. Why should she pick up after herself? "I know what I'll do," the princess said to herself. "I'll teach everyone a lesson. I'll run away from home and leave my room messed up just like this." She searched through her dresser drawers for old clothing, pitching what she did not want on the floor. Finding the clothing she wanted to dress up in, she disguised herself as one of the village peasant girls. Then, she quietly slipped out of the castle's secret door.

The princess knew her father, the King, would not discover her missing for several hours because he was attending to important business.

Walking a short distance, the princess soon found herself in a neighborhood lined with markets and merchants. On a narrow backstreet she met a group of children playing stickball. She thought to herself, "They are having much more fun than I ever have. I'm tired of being a princess. I shall be like them."

It wasn't long before the children asked her to play stickball with them. She was so happy. The princess quickly caught on to their game. She elbowed whoever got in her way…just like them. She cursed when she missed the ball…just like them. And when she fell, plop, she fell straight into the mud…just like them.

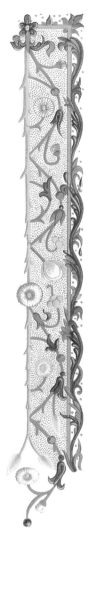

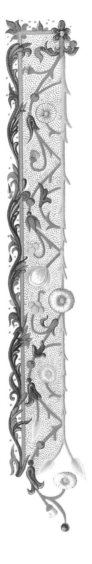

Suddenly a young girl appeared at the corner of the street. She called to the children, "Come, hurry, something really big is happening on Main Street." Sticks flew into the air and the children ran toward Main Street. The princess was quite proud of herself for she could run very fast…just like them.

When the children reached Main Street, they reached a crowd of people who were oohing and ahhing over something. The children shoved and pushed their way through the crowd only to meet the stares of the finely dressed men and women standing at the front of the group. "Go away, you filthy children," one woman said. Incensed the princess said, "I am no filthy child. I am a prin…" Her words trailed off. Looking at the children standing around her, she thought to herself, "I used to be a princess. Now I'm just like them!" With new resolve she began to elbow her way through the crowd again, purposely getting mud on the hems of the fine dresses and skirts.

"It's no use," one of the boys finally said, "We can't get to the front of this crowd. Hurry, let's go climb that tree over there." The children hurried to the tree and just like monkeys scurried up to perch on the branches. All the children managed to climb the tree, except for the princess. Trailing behind them she reassured herself, "I can climb this tree…I can because I'm just like them." As she pulled her way to the second branch, a small limb caught the threads of her skirt and threw her off balance. Not being able to catch herself, she tumbled out of the tree and fell to the ground with a thump. The adults turned around and peered at her with disgust. The children in the tree laughed and yelled at her, "Get up here, quick. It's coming, it's coming." She didn't know what was coming, nor did she care at this particular moment. Humiliated and bruised from the fall, she wanted to cry. But she was like them and they certainly wouldn't cry. So, she cursed instead.

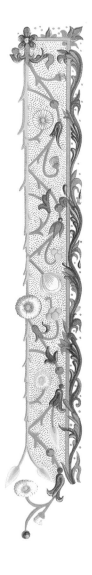

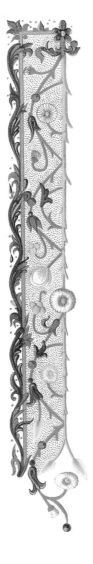

Determined, the princess finally made her way up the tree and settled insecurely on a lower branch. "What are we looking for anyway?" she asked.

"It's the King," yelled the other kids. "Don't you know a King when you see one," they sneered at her. She slowly pulled herself up to the next branch and stretched to see the King. An envoy of dignitaries stood beside a lavish coach. When the door opened, out stepped the King. So tall. So dignified. So royal! "Hail, His Majesty the King," an aide announced. The crowd responded, "Long live the King." The dignitaries dropped to one knee. The crowd bowed before him. Only the King was left standing.

Then one of the boys in the tree whispered to the group, "Hey, we have a perfect shot from here. Let's throw our best spitballs right in his face." Horror struck the princess' heart. "You can't do that," she pleaded.

"Why not?" the boys demanded.

"Because he's the King," she said.

"So, what. Big deal," they said as they began to throw spitballs at the King.

"Stop," the princess cried. "Stop please. That's my father." The tears she had so valiantly held back earlier now spilled down her cheeks.

"Sure, and my dad is Abraham," they mocked her.

"No, I mean it. It's true. The King is my father," she pleaded. But the children just laughed harder.

"Look at you. You're just like us," they sneered. "You don't have a father."

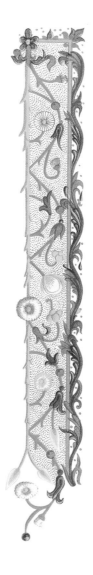

The princess looked at her father just in time to see him wipe something from his face. He looked up into the tree as the children yelled and cursed at him. Indescribable shame filled her heart. She was sure her father had seen her. But maybe, just maybe, he hadn't recognized her. The princess jumped out of the tree and began to run. As she did, the children started to throw their spitballs at her. The princess began to run back toward the palace. She ran and ran, sobbing every step of the way. Stopping to catch her breath the princess suddenly became aware of her stinging elbows and knees. She was skinned and bleeding from the fall and she began to cry even harder. Her heart sank and she felt alone and very frightened.

Making her way slowly back to the palace she discovered, to her horror, that the secret door was now locked. She ran to the next door, but it was locked too. As was the next and the next door. "Oh, no!" she cried, "I am locked out and have no place to go. The palace is no longer my home." The princess knew that only the front door remained – unlocked. "I can't possibly use the front door," she thought, "everyone will know how foolish I have been. Everyone will look at me…and I look just like them."

So she waited and waited, trying desperately to think of some way to get out of this terrible mess. Finally, too sore and too hungry to think any longer, she gave in and headed for the front door. With torn clothes, filthy hands, and a tear-streaked face, she lifted her hand and knocked once, slowly, timidly. Before she could muster the courage to knock again the door cracked open. Hanging her head in shame, she could see only his feet. But she knew instantly that they were his feet. It was him. Her dad. Her father. The King. She fell at his feet and cried, "I'm sorry Daddy. I am so ashamed of what I have done."

Gently, the King knelt down beside her and pulled her into his strong, comforting arms. "Come here, my child, my princess," he said.

"But I'm not a princess any more...I'm just like them," she sobbed.

"Ah, my child," he said. "You may have acted like them, but you are not one of them. You are mine, and you will never be happy until you accept both the privilege and responsibility that goes with belonging to me."

25

That night, after he had dressed her wounds, he tucked her into her soft bed and kissed her goodnight. He had even helped her to clean the mess she had left in her room. As she settled into the soft quilts, she thought about how much she liked being a princess, the daughter of a King.

As the King walked out of the room, the dim night light softly illuminated his royal robe, which was now smudged with dirt. Tears filled the princess' eyes, "Look what I've done to the King's robe. Never again," she whispered, apologizing to the King.

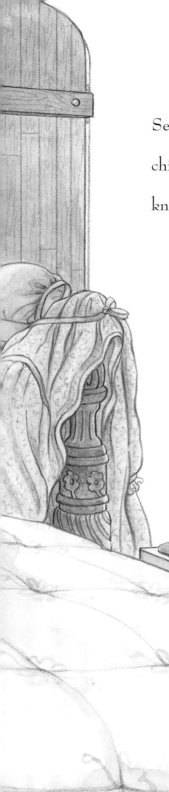

Sensing her broken heart, the King turned and spoke softly, "Yes, my child, there will be other times, but I will open the door every time you knock and I will always love you...ever, again."

And this story has no end.

29

"Come, you who are blessed by my Father;

take your inheritance,

the kingdom prepared for you

since the creation of the world."

MATTHEW 25:34B